Nelson
Handwriting

Developing Skills

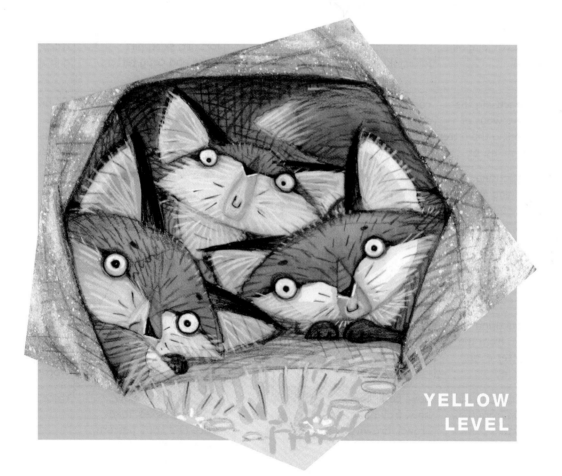

YELLOW LEVEL

Anita Warwick

Series editor: John Jackman

CONTENTS/SCOPE AND SEQUENCE

Further practice of the four handwriting joins.

Page	Focus	Extra	Extension	Focus resource	Extension resource
4-5 Unit 1 First join revision	revising the first join: in, ine	pine, dine	choose words and copy sentences	in, bin, din, pin trace and copy pattern and words, trace and copy sentence	(magic e words) pin, pine, din, dine, hid, hide, pip, pipe, shin, shine, slim, slime trace and copy words
6-7 Unit 2 Second join revision	revising the second join: ut, ute	tube, cube, cute	choose words and copy sentences	ub, tub, cub, ut, but, put, hut, cut trace and copy pattern and words	(magic e words) tub, tube, cub, cube, cut, cute trace and copy words and sentence
8-9 Unit 3 Third join revision	revising the third join: ve, vi	cave, caving, save, saving, wave, waving	choose words and copy sentences	ve, very, over, we, were, went, re, tree, three trace and copy letters and words	we, were, ve, very, fe, feet, trace and copy letters, words and sentence
10-11 Unit 4 Fourth join revision	revising the fourth join: ok, oh	choke, choking, smoke, smoking, joke, joking	choose words and copy sentences	oke, joke, ole, hole, ort, fort, irt, skirt, dirt trace and copy letters and words	poked, poking trace and copy words and sentence
12-13 Unit 5 Secrets	practising the two ways of joining the letter s: sh, as, es	code, codes, ship, ships, message, messages	choose words and copy sentences	sh, es, shines, shoes, shapes, shaves, shoves, shares trace and copy pattern, letters and words	us, house, as, has, ds, dads, es, gates trace and copy letters, words and sentence
14-15 Unit 6 Secrets	practising joining from the letter r: ri, ru, ry	trick, trust, try	choose words and copy sentences	ri, trip, triangle, ru, true, truth, ry, cry trace and copy pattern, letters and words	ru, trunk, ry, carry, ri, carries trace and copy letters, words and sentence
16-17 Unit 7 Roads	practising the join to and from the letter a: oa, ad, as	load, road, toad, boat, goat, coat, toast, roast, boast	copy poem	oa, soap, ad, had, as, has, gas, last trace and copy pattern, letters and words	goat, coat, boat, afloat trace and copy words and sentence
18-19 Unit 8 Roads	practising the join from the letter e: ee, ea, ed	see, bee, fee, seed, need feed, sea, pea, flea	copy poem	ee, bee, tree, three, ea, beach, peach, teach trace and copy patten, letters and words	ea, ear, eat, meat, eals, meals, eas, peas trace and copy, letters, words and sentence
20-21 Unit 9 Animals	practising the join from the letter o: ow, ov, ox	bow, cow, how, now, frown, brown, crown, drown ox, pox, box, fox	match questions to answer and copy jokes	ow, cow, now, how, bow, ox, boxes, foxes trace and copy pattern, letters and words	trace and copy poem
22-23 Unit 10 Animals	practising joining to the letter y: ky, hy, ly	sly, fly ply sky, spy, shy high, higher, highest	copy poem	ky, milky, silky, hy healthy, wealthy, ly, jolly, dolly trace and copy pattern, letters and words	ay, Monday, Tuesday, Wednesday, Thursday, Friday, Saturday, Sunday, January, February, May, July
24-25 Check-up 1	Check-up	Check-up	Check-up	Check-up	Check-up

Page	Focus	Extra	Extension	Focus resource	Extension resource
26-27 Unit 11 Woods	practising joining to the letter a: ha, ta, fa	hair, hare, fair, fare stair, stare, pair, pare	choose words and copy sentences	ha, hail, hailstorm ta, tail, tailor, fa, fail trace and copy pattern, letters and words	trace and copy sentences
28-29 Unit 12 Woods	practising joining from the letter o: od, oo, og	good, hood, wood book, took, look dog, hog, log	choose words and copy sentences	od, nod, rod, og, bog, frog, oo, cook trace and copy pattern, letters and words	trace and copy poem
30-31 Unit 13 Reptiles	practising joining to the letter r: er, ir, ur	sister, mister, blister, bird, dirt, shirt hurt, hurtle, turtle	copy poem	er, her, ir, stir, third, ur, burn, turn trace and copy pattern, letters and words	trace and copy poem
32-33 Unit 14 Reptiles	practising the first and second join join: ai, al, ay	tail, sail, pail tale, sale, pale, tray, stray, play	choose words and copy sentences	ai, rain, again, al, ball, call, ay, may, stay trace and copy pattern, letters and words	copy poem
34-35 Unit 15 Bridges	practising joining from the letter o: oy, ou, oi	speech marks and apostrophes	copy sentences	oi, oil, soil, spoil, oy, joy, coy, boy	speech marks and apostrophes, copy words and sentences
36-37 Unit 16 Transport	practising the horizontal join to the letter e: re, oe, fe	toe, foe, woe fear, dear, year dream, cream, stream	copy poem	re, there, where, oe, Zoe, Chloe, fe, feet, feed Trace and copy pattern, letters and words	trace and copy letters, words and sentence
38-39 Unit 17 People	practising the horizontal join to the letter u: fu, wu, vu	care, careful, carefully, help, helpful, helpfully, wonder, wonderful, wonderfully	choose word and copy sentences	fu, fun, funny, wu, swum, swung, vu, vulture trace and copy pattern, letters and words	copy poem
40-41 Unit 18 People	practising print: copy print letters	arm, hair, hand, knee, thumb, eye, fingers, foot, shoulder, leg, wrist, mouth	draw and label picture	copy print letters	copy print words, label parts of dog
42-43 Unit 19 Weather	practising joining to ascenders: ot, ol, ok	not, hot, rot, blot, got, cot, dot, spot	copy poem	ot, soot, foot, ol, fool, cool, ok, hook, book trace and copy pattern, letters and words	make and add 'ing' to words copy sentence
44-45 Unit 20 Weather	practising all the joins: ai, al, ow, ol	raindrop, rainbow, rainfall	make and copy compound words	ai, hail, al, fall, ow, snow, ol, cold trace and copy pattern, letters and words	copy poem
46-48 Check-up 2	*Check-up*	*Check-up*	*Check-up*	*Check-up*	*Check-up*

Revising the first join.

in

Playing in the line.

F OCUS

A Copy this pattern into your book.

B Copy these letters into your book.

in in in in in

ine ine ine ine ine

Remember, the first join is made by joining the bottom of one letter to the top of the next, like this:

i + n = in

 **XTRA**

Make these words.
Copy them into your book.

pin + e = pine pine pine

din + e = dine dine dine

 **XTENSION**

Choose the correct words to finish the sentences.
Copy the sentences into your book.

1 Ben used a (pin / pine).

2 Pug made a (din / dine).

Revising the second join.

ut

Ruby has a cut.

FOCUS

A Copy this pattern into your book.

B Copy these letters into your book.

ut ut ut ut ut

ute ute ute ute ute

Remember, the second join is made by taking your pencil from the bottom of one letter up to the top of the next, like this:

u + t = ut

Make these words.
Copy them into your book.

tub + e = tube tube tube

cub + e = cube cube cube

cut + e = cute cute cute

XTENSION

Choose the correct words to finish these sentences.
Copy the sentences into your book.

1 Ruby (cut/cute) her knee.

2 Her mum used a (tub/tube).

3 Ruby held her (cub/cube).

Revising the third join.

ve

They waved and waved.

Focus

A Copy this pattern into your book.

VV VV VV VV

B Copy these letters into your book.

ve ve ve ve ve
vi vi vi vi vi

Remember, the third join is a horizontal join between two letters, like this:

v + e = ve

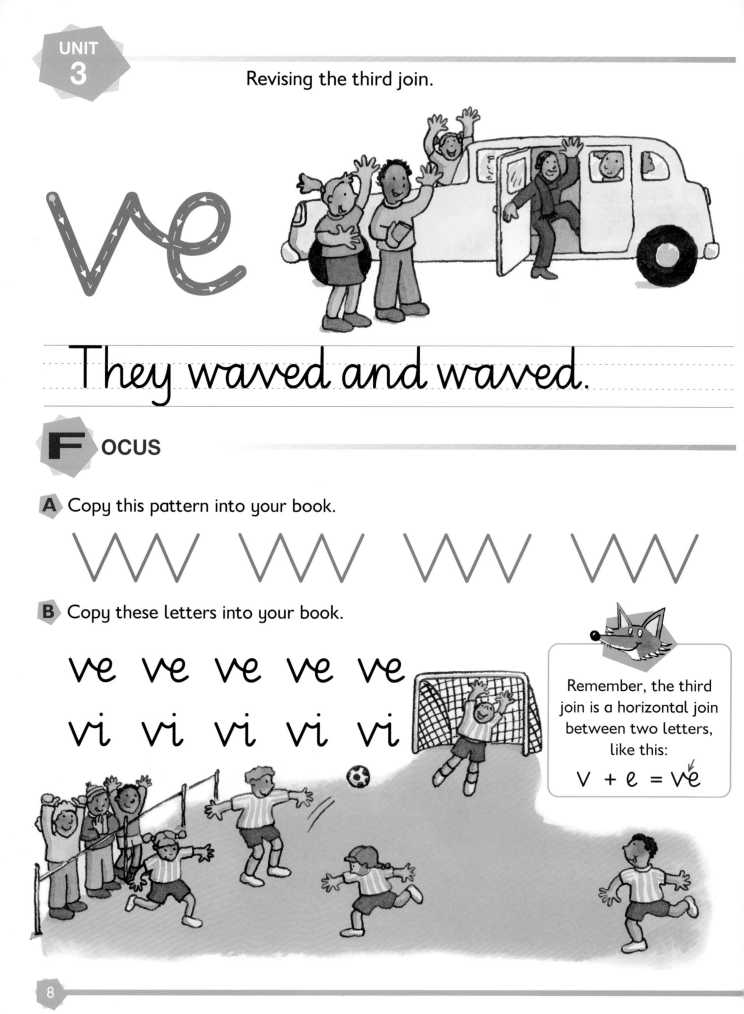

 **EXTRA**

Make these words. Copy them into your book.
Remember to drop the letter *e* when adding *ing*.

cave + ing = caving   caving

save + ing = saving   saving

wave + ing = waving   waving

E **XTENSION**

Choose the correct word from the **Extra** above to finish these sentences.
Copy the sentences into your book.

1 The family went _____ .

2 They saw a man in
the sea _____ .

3 They saw the lifeguard
_____ him.

Revising the fourth join.

ok

Stoke the fire to make it smoke.

FOCUS

A Copy this pattern into your book.

olol olol olol olol

B Copy these letters into your book.

ok ok ok ok ok

oh oh oh oh oh

Remember, the fourth join is made by joining the top of one letter to the top of another, like this:

o + k = ok

 **XTRA**

Make these words. Copy them into your book.
Remember to drop the letter *e* when adding *ing*.

choke + ing = choking   choking

smoke + ing = smoking   smoking

joke + ing   = joking   joking

XTENSION

Choose the correct words to finish these sentences.
Copy the sentences into your book.

1 Sita said she could see
(smoke/smoking).

2 They thought Sita
was (joke/joking).

3 People were
(choke/choking).

Practising the two ways of joining the letter **s**.

sh es

Jess shares her secret.

FOCUS

A Copy this pattern into your book.

B Copy these letters into your book.

sh sh sh sh sh

as as as as as

es es es es es

S is used at the start of
a word or after a break
letter, like this:
shops
s is used within words,
like this:
messages

SHOE SHOP

12

EXTRA

Make these words.
Copy them into your book.

code + s   = codes   codes

ship + s   = ships   ships

message + s = messages messages

EXTENSION

Choose the correct word to finish these sentences.
Copy the sentences into your book.

1 Some people use code when they send (message/messages).

2 Morse Code was used by (ship/ships).

3 Morse (Code/Codes) was invented by Samuel Morse.

Practising joining from the letter **r**.

ri

Terri tried to keep the secret.

FOCUS

A Copy this pattern into your book.

B Copy these letters into your book.

ri ri ri ri ri

ru ru ru ru ru

ry ry ry ry ry

Remember, the letter y has a descender. Its tail goes below the line.

 **XTRA**

Copy these words into your book.

trick trick trick trick

trust trust trust trust

try   try   try   try

EXTENSION

Choose the correct word from the **Extra** above to finish these sentences.
Copy the sentences into your book.

Question marks are as tall as an ascender.

1 I know a _____ .

2 Do you want to _____ it?

3 Can I _____ you to keep it a secret?

oa

Take care crossing the road.

FOCUS

A Copy this pattern into your book.

B Copy these letters into your book.

oa oa oa oa oa

ad ad ad ad ad

as as as as as

16

EXTRA

Copy these words into your book.

load	boat	toast
road	coat	roast
toad	goat	boast

EXTENSION

A Copy this poem into your book.

Green toad
Black road
Red lorry
Large load
Green road
No toad.

'*Green Toad*' by *Constance Milburn*

Remember,
the joins help you to
keep the correct space
between your letters.

B Underline all the words with **oa** in them.

17

Practising the join from the letter **e**.

Hear the beat of feet on the street.

FOCUS

A Copy this pattern into your book.

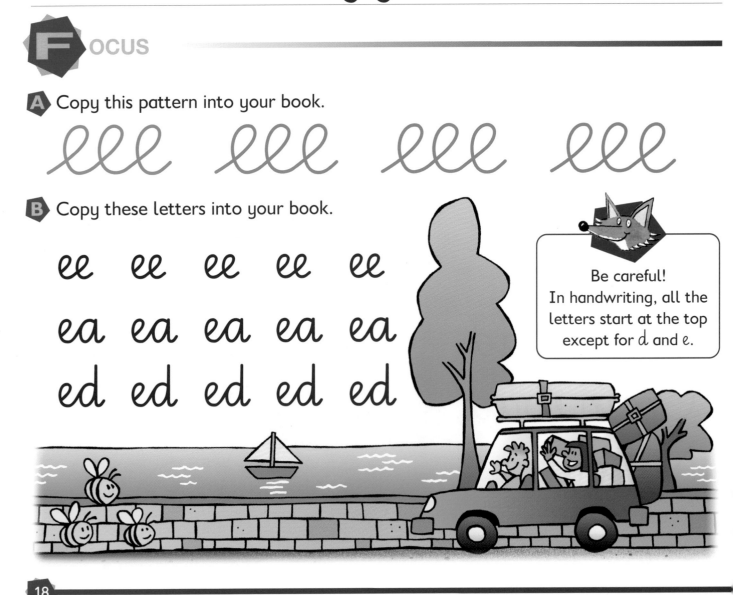

B Copy these letters into your book.

ee ee ee ee ee

ea ea ea ea ea

ed ed ed ed ed

Be careful!
In handwriting, all the
letters start at the top
except for d and e.

Copy these words into your book.

see	seed	sea
bee	need	pea
fee	feed	flea

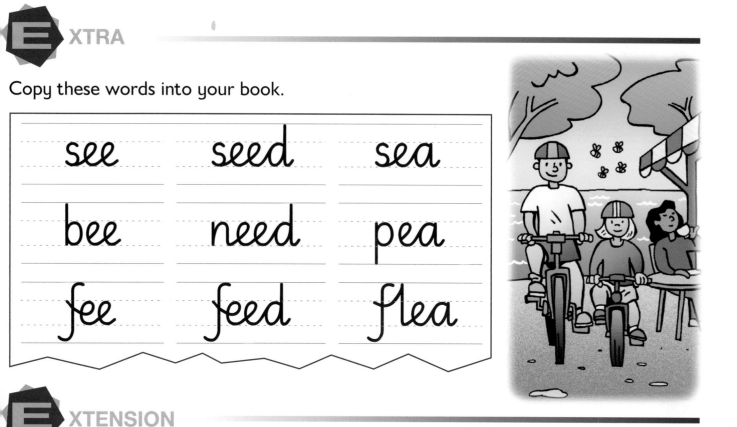

EXTENSION

Copy this poem into your book.

Hurry, scurry: lock that door –
this poor car will take no more!
Hurry scurry; turn the key,
We're off at last to see the sea.

from *'All Aboard'* by *Judith Nicholls*

Practising the join from the letter **o**.

OW

How now brown cow.

Focus

A Copy this pattern into your book.

ovov ovov ovov ovov

B Copy these letters into your book.

ow ow ow ow ow

ov ov ov ov ov

ox ox ox ox ox

Remember,
the joining line helps
you leave the correct
space between your
letters.

E XTRA

Copy these words into your book.

bow	frown	ox
cow	brown	pox
how	crown	box
now	drown	fox

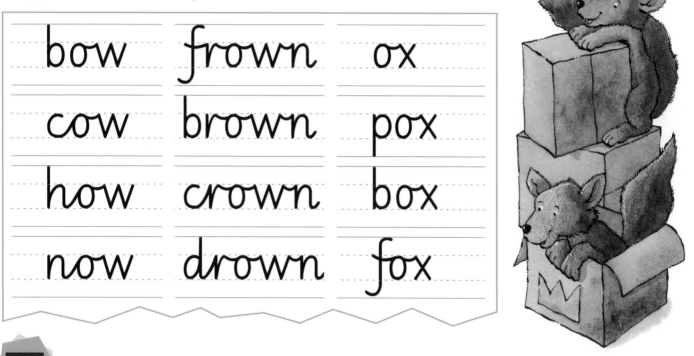

E XTENSION

Match the questions below to the answers in the box.
Copy the correct jokes into your book.

> Chick to chick   A milk shake

1 How do hens dance?
2 What do you get from a nervous cow?

Practising joining to the letter **y**.

ky

The kangaroos jump in the sky.

FOCUS

A Copy this pattern into your book.

B Copy these letters into your book.

ky ky ky ky ky
hy hy hy hy hy
ly ly ly ly ly

Remember,
the letter y has a
descender. Its tail goes
below the line.

Copy these words into your book.

ly	y	igh
sly	sky	high
fly	spy	higher
ply	shy	highest

EXTENSION

Copy this poem into your book.

Flapping by
In the midnight sky.
Higher and higher –
See him fly!
See him fly!

Remember,
the letters f, p, g and y
all have descenders.
Their tails go below
the line.

CHECK-UP 1

FOCUS

Copy these patterns into your book.

EXTRA

Copy these words into your book.

dine pine see seed

cube tube ship ships

caving waving code codes

joke joking choke choking

EXTENSION

Copy the poem below into your book.

As I was walking up the stair
I met a man who wasn't there;
He wasn't there again today.
I wish, I wish he'd stay away.

'The Little Man'
by *Hughes Mearns*

Practising joining to the letter **a**.

ha

A pair of hares in the dark.

FOCUS

A Copy this pattern into your book.

lclc lclc lclc lclc

B Copy these letters into your book.

ha ha ha ha ha
ta ta ta ta ta
fa fa fa fa fa

Remember,
the letter t is not as
tall as the other letters
with ascenders.

Copy these words into your book.

hair hare fair fare

stair stare pair pare

EXTENSION

Homophones are words that sound the same but are spelt differently.
Use one of the homophones to fill each gap. Copy the sentences into your book.

1 fair fare   Aisha and Spot were going to the _____ .

2 hair hare   Spot chased a _____ in the woods.

3 stair stare   Aisha tried not to _____ at the mess.

Practising joining from the letter **o**.

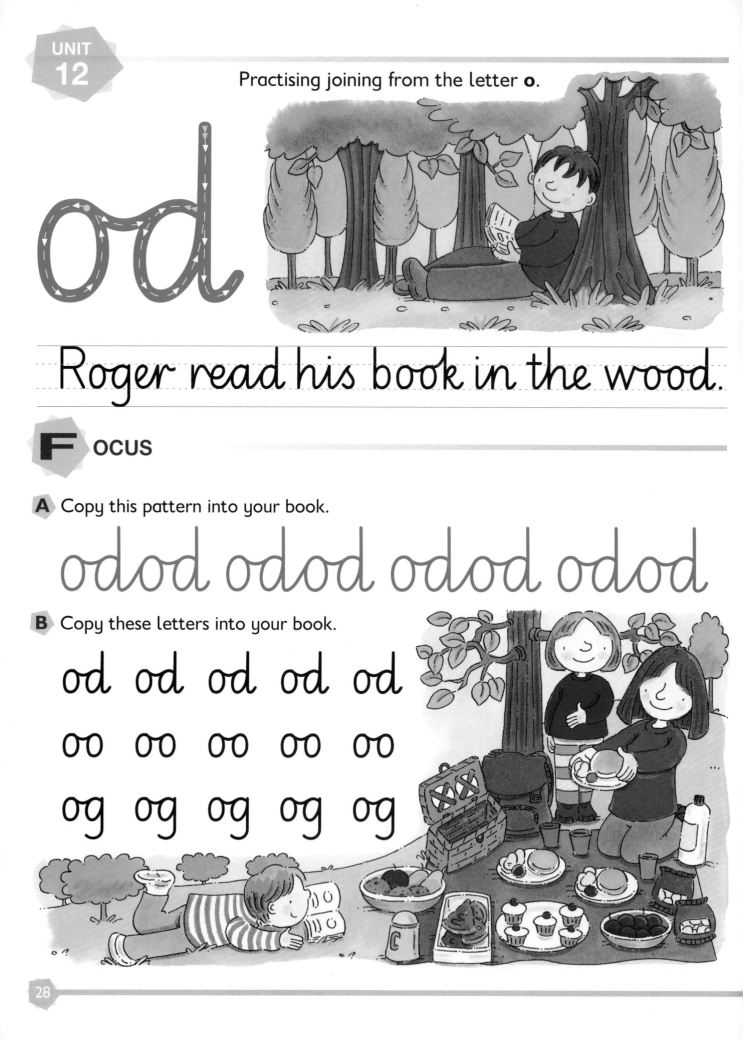

od

Roger read his book in the wood.

FOCUS

A Copy this pattern into your book.

odod odod odod odod

B Copy these letters into your book.

od od od od od

oo oo oo oo oo

og og og og og

Copy these words into your book.

good	book	dog
hood	took	hog
wood	look	log

E **XTENSION**

Choose the correct word to fill the gaps.
Copy the sentences into your book.

1 **Hood wood** Little Red Riding ____ walked through the ____ to visit her grandmother.

2 **book took** She ____ some food and a ____ with her.

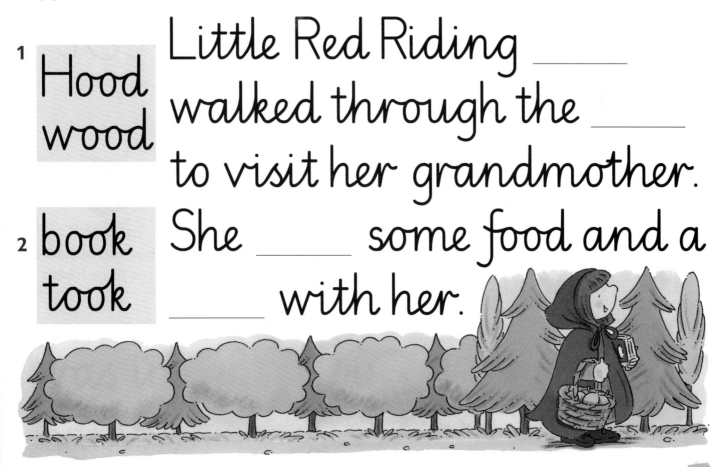

Practising joining to the letter **r**.

er

Slippery, slithery, sliding snake.

FOCUS

A Copy this pattern into your book.

B Copy these letters into your book.

er er er er er

ir ir ir ir ir

ur ur ur ur ur

Be careful!
These letters should all
be the same height.

EXTRA

Copy these words into your book.

er	ir	ur
sister	bird	hurt
mister	dirt	hurtle
blister	shirt	turtle

EXTENSION

Copy this poem into your book.

A rabbit raced a turtle,

You know the turtle won;

And Mister Bunny came in late

A little hot cross bun!

Anonymous

Practising the first and second join.

ai

Jake the snake. Gail the snail.

Focus

A Copy this pattern into your book.

aiai aiai aiai aiai

B Copy these letters into your book.

ai ai ai ai ai

al al al al al

ay ay ay ay ay

Remember to leave the correct space between your letters.

Copy these words into your book.

tail	tale	tray
sail	sale	stray
pail	pale	play

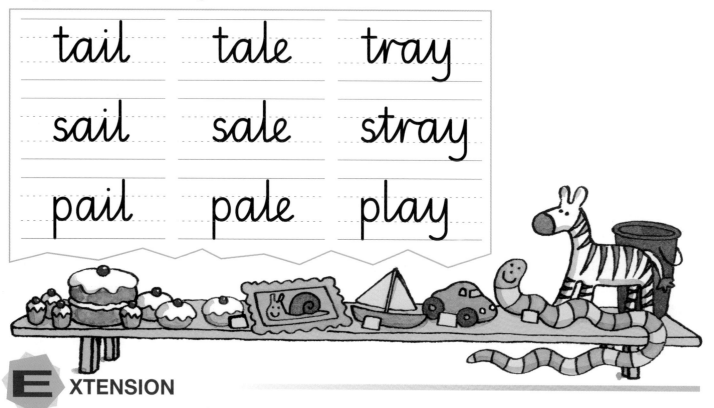

E XTENSION

Use your dictionary to decide which is the correct homophone for each sentence. Copy the sentences into your book.

1 The gecko had a long (tail/tale).

2 Hayley asked if the tortoise was for (sail/sale).

3 The man turned (pail/pale) as the snake slid towards him.

Practising joining from the letter **o**.

oy

The boys point to a coin.

FOCUS

A Copy this pattern into your book.

oioy oioy oioy oioy

B Copy these letters into your book.

oy oy oy oy oy

ou ou ou ou ou

oi oi oi oi oi

A Speech marks are used to show words that are being spoken. They are written using short strokes and should be at the same height as the tops of the ascenders. Copy the sentence into your book.

"Look out," shouted the boy.

B Apostrophes are similar to speech marks. They are used when a letter is missed out. Make these words. Copy them into your book.

who + is = who's

do + not = don't

EXTENSION

Copy these sentences into your book.

1 "Who lives under the bridge?" asked the boy.

2 "Don't shout or the troll will jump out," replied Little Billy Goat Gruff.

Practising the horizontal join to the letter **e**.

re

Are you ready?

FOCUS

A Copy this pattern into your book.

rere rere rere rere

B Copy these letters into your book.

re re re re re

oe oe oe oe oe

fe fe fe fe fe

Copy these words into your book.

toe	fear	dream
foe	dear	cream
woe	year	stream

Make sure you write the letter e correctly, like this:

oe ✗   oe ✓

EXTENSION

Copy this poem into your book.

Fingers grip,
toes curl;
head down,
wheels whirl.

Hair streams,
fields race;
ears sting,
winds chase.

from 'Biking' by Judith Nicholls

Practising the horizontal join to the letter u.

fu

My friends are full of fun.

FOCUS

A Copy this pattern into your book.

vwu vwu vwu vwu

B Copy these letters into your book.

fu fu fu fu fu

wu wu wu wu wu

vu vu vu vu vu

Be careful!
f is a tall letter. It has
a straight back.

Copy these words into your book.

care   careful   carefully

help   helpful   helpfully

wonder wonderful wonderfully

EXTENSION

Choose the correct word to finish these sentences.
Copy the sentences into your book.

1 Trisha's mum (care/ careful/carefully) helped the children cross the road.

2 The dinner lady told Alison's teacher she had been a big (help/ helpful/helpfully) at lunchtime.

Practising printing.

print

Cinderella
Date: 16th May
Time: 5pm
At:
Marshfield
School

FOCUS

Copy the print letters into your book.

a b c d e f g h i j k l m

n o p q r s t u v w x y z

 **EXTRA**

Copy the printed words into your book.

arm   hair   hand   knee

thumb   eye   fingers   foot

shoulder   leg   wrist   mouth

E **XTENSION**

A Draw a picture of a friend.

B Print the labels from the **Extra** onto your picture.
Two labels are done to help you.

arm

knee

Practising joining to ascenders.

ot

I'm in a hot spot.

F OCUS

A Copy this pattern into your book.

okok okok okok okok

B Copy these letters into your book.

ot   ot   ot   ot   ot

ol   ol   ol   ol   ol

ok   ok   ok   ok   ok

Copy these words into your book.

not	hot	rot	blot
got	cot	dot	spot

Remember,
the letter t is not as
tall as an ascender.

EXTENSION

Copy the poem into your book.

I'm looking for a hot spot
To hit a ball and run.
Oh, I'm looking for a hot spot.
A what spot?
A hot spot.
I'm looking for a hot spot
Now summer has begun.

from *'Summer Days'* by Anne English

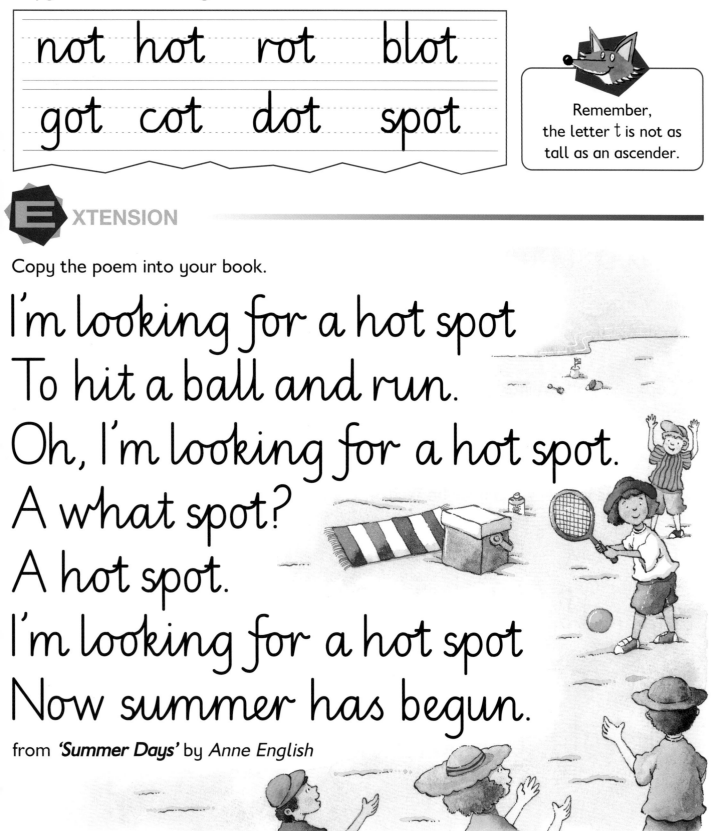

ai
oi al
ow

Sally tried to follow the rainbow.

FOCUS

A Copy this pattern into your book.

aowl aowl aowl aowl

B Copy these letters into your book.

ai ai ai ai ai

al al al al al

ow ow ow ow ow

oi oi oi oi oi

A compound word is made from two small words added together.
Copy these compound words into your book.

rain + drop = raindrop

rain + bow = rainbow

rain + fall = rainfall

EXTENSION

A Look at the words in the box.

thunder cloud bolt
storm   drops rain

Use them to make six compound words.
Write them into your book.

B How many compound words can you make using the word *snow*?
Write them into your book.

FOCUS

Copy these patterns into your book.

icic icic icic icic

odod odod odod odod

eiei eiei eiei eiei

oioy oioy oioy oioy

vwu vwu vwu vwu

aowl aowl aowl aowl

Copy the words into your book.

dear hear help helpful

tail tale sail sale

fare fair foe woe

look took dirt shirt

Copy the poem into your book.

Today I saw a little worm,
Wriggling on his belly.
Perhaps he'd like to come inside,
And see what's on the telly?

'The Worm' by *Spike Milligan*